OVERCOMING
THE WORLD

Faith Cook

ET Perspectives No. 4

Published by
EVANGELICAL TIMES
Faverdale North, Darlington, DL3 0PH, England

E-mail: theeditors@evangelicaltimes.org

Web: http://www.evangelicaltimes.org

First published 2007

British Library Cataloguing in Publication Data available

ISBN 0-9500129-4-7

Printed in Great Britain
by Athenaeum Press, Gateshead, UK

Other titles in the ET Perspectives series are;
1. *Preaching Christ* by Edgar Andrews
2. *Heaven* by Gordon Keddie
3. *A Cloud of Witnesses* by Michael Haykin
Obtainable from bookshops or from
sales@evangelicalpress.org

TITLE

CONTENTS page

Publisher's Note

From time to time, *Evangelical Times*, a monthly newspaper, publishes series of articles on a variety of subjects, ranging from historical to theological, from practical Christian living to Bible exposition. The Editors feel that these series are often of sufficient interest to warrant being made available in their own right, and have therefore launched a series of booklets under the generic title ET Perspectives as a means to this end.

The main chapters of this booklet first appeared as a series of articles in *Evangelical Times* over several years from 1999 to 2006. All this material now appears in collected form as the fourth volume of ET Perspectives.

Our prayerful hope is that these inexpensive booklets will be of use in furthering the gospel of the glory of our Lord Jesus Christ and bringing men and women to a deeper knowledge of his unsearchable riches.

The Editors
Evangelical Times

Author's Preface

A search among the headstones in an old cemetery for evidences of godly men and women of bygone days, can be both disappointing and encouraging. Often it yields little apart from some semi-legible platitudes on lichen-covered graves. Then occasionally one discovers a gem. When Eliza Crow died in 1757 at the age of forty-seven, her friends described her as having possessed:

> *Sarah's obedience, Lydia's open heart,*
> *Martha's care but Mary's better part.*

Clearly Eliza was a woman whose pattern of life was marked by a humble walk with God.

People sometimes ask me how I set about choosing a person to write about in a collection such as this. Like the search among the old headstones, it is not always easy to find suitable characters. Occasionally I come across some long-forgotten Christian in the course of my reading — one whose life is well-worth remembering. But this is not the only criterion. Perhaps a better clue lies in the title of this ET Perspectives booklet, Overcoming the world.

It is often those who have struggled and overcome by the help of God — those who have battled on in the face of weakness and need — who have most appealed to me. These men and women have become noteworthy, not primarily because of great natural gifts, but because of the enabling grace of God.

In some cases their triumphs have been won in extreme circumstances, even through the pains of martyrdom. But more often the accounts from the past that have grabbed my interest are of those who felt their vulnerability and limitations — whose sins have cast them into despair, yet who have 'cried out to the

Lord in their trouble' (Psalm 107:19). These are the ones whose faith 'overcomes the world' (1 John 5:4).

As the editors point out, these chapters are culled from past issues of Evangelical Times, a journal that has celebrated forty years of publication. They represent a typical range of such subjects — an ex-slave girl who would prefer to die than continue under the burden of a guilty conscience; a missionary who fears he has spent his strength in an unavailing cause, but is so wrong; a man of courage who perished in the fires of Mary Tudor's fanaticism; and perhaps my heroine among women, Selina, Countess of Huntingdon, whose life-long accomplishments were set against a backdrop of physical weakness and personal bereavement. Lastly, there is a reminder of the life of Fred Mitchell — once a household name among evangelical Christians.

I am most grateful to the editors of Evangelical Times, Edgar Andrews and Roger Fay, for their invaluable help in editing and improving my articles, not to forget the earlier work of scrutiny on the part of my husband, Paul.

I hope that this small book will encourage its readers in the spiritual fight to 'overcome the world', for we live in days of rampant ungodliness, with the possibility of persecution for those of steadfast Christian principle looming ever nearer. May we be among that number who 'did not love their lives to the death' but 'overcame by the blood of the Lamb and by the word of their testimony' (Revelation 12:11).

Faith Cook

1. Overcoming martyrdom

John Rogers

At a time when Christians worldwide are experiencing high levels of persecution and maltreatment, with martyrdoms ever on the increase, it is right to remember the grievous sufferings of those who perished during the reign of Mary Tudor. Almost three hundred men and women would die at the stake, the first being John Rogers — whose name should never be forgotten. Born in 1500, his life spanned a mere fifty-five years — yet it still shines like a beacon, lighting our uncertain pathway through a third millennium.

John Rogers' childhood days, spent near Birmingham, gave little indication of what he would one day become. Like other well-placed youths he attended university, studying classics at Pembroke Hall, Cambridge; but not until 1532 do we have any other definite indications of his movements.

By this time he had become a typical clergyman of the day, responsible for a City of London church. With no strong convictions of his own, he followed the prevailing currents of thought. He was certainly no friend of the Reformers — men like Martin Luther, John Knox and William Tyndale — whose work was shaking the old order of things.

But God had his hand on this undistinguished, though able, cleric. Two years later he relinquished his London church and sailed for Antwerp. There he became chaplain to the English residents, some of whom were exiles for conscience sake, hounded from their homes by Henry VIII's zealous Chancellor Sir Thomas More.

The Bible in English

Before long he came across one exile — a Gloucestershire man whose labours seemed shrouded in secrecy — named William Tyndale. Toiling incessantly on his translation of the Old Testament from Hebrew into English, Tyndale seemed to sense that his time was short.

With his translation of the New Testament already completed and circulating clandestinely throughout England, he knew that Sir Thomas More's spies could discover his hiding place at any time. And then all opportunity to finish his great work would be at an end. Already his friend and helper John Fryth had been caught and cruelly martyred.

So now, when Tyndale discovered that the young English chaplain was schooled in Greek and Hebrew, he took a calculated risk. He sought Rogers' help in this last great work of translation.

With no 'heart religion', Rogers approached the Scriptures with an academic's mind, being pleased to put his Greek and Hebrew to use once more. But God's time had come for the young man. As he pored over the Hebrew text, labouring diligently alongside Tyndale, the Word of God began to cast its radiant light into his mind.

The truth took hold of him and transformed his thinking. Now he saw everything from a new perspective. 'I have found the true light in the gospel', he declared to Tyndale one day. Delivered from the heavy yoke of formal religion, and a slavish adherence to the traditions of the Church, John Rogers became a new man in Christ.

In every town and hamlet

Only a few months later, Tyndale was caught at last. Treacherously betrayed by one he had innocently trusted, a certain Henry Phillips, he was arrested and thrown into a cold, dank prison. He never emerged again except to face a fiery martyrdom. Rogers, meanwhile, pressed on with Tyndale's unfinished manuscript, adding to it the work of another translator, Miles Coverdale, to complete the Old Testament. Even before Tyndale was martyred, the entire English Bible was circulating secretly in his homeland.

'Lord, open the king of England's eyes', Tyndale had prayed as he died, and within a year of his death that prayer was abundantly answered. A copy of the Scriptures, allegedly the work of a Thomas Matthews, came into the king's hands. Carefully he examined the neat volume. Discovering no mention of the name 'William Tyndale', and approving the respectfully written dedication, the king made an unexpected and momentous decision. Across the title-page he wrote, 'Set forth with the King's most gracious licence'.

'Matthew's Bible' as it was called was in reality Tyndale's work with Coverdale's additions, finalised by John Rogers and printed under the pseudonym of Thomas Matthews. Now the completed Bible could be distributed openly in every town and hamlet in England.

Severe setback

To John Rogers had fallen this undoubted privilege, but God had a yet higher honour in store for the Antwerp chaplain. After marrying a Dutch girl, Adriana de Wayden, Rogers moved to the relative safety of Luther's Wittenberg, where his numerous family was born.

He acted as pastor to a German congregation for the next ten years until 1547, the year that Henry VIII died and the boy king Edward VI came to the throne. Circumstances were now highly favourable to the progress of the Reformation, and John Rogers was anxious to serve God in his own land once more.

Rogers' faithful and courageous preaching brought him to the attention of Nicholas Ridley, then Bishop of London. Recognising his abilities and zeal, Ridley appointed him to a prominent London pulpit within the deanery of St. Paul's.

But only three years later the young king died and his half-sister Mary Tudor came to the throne. Never had the work of the English Reformation suffered so severe a setback as in the grievous years that followed. Mary determined to reverse all the reforms brought in during her brother's reign. But God had

his men, resolute, faithful and determined — men who believed the Word of God with every fibre of their being — and were prepared to die for it if need be.

John Rogers dared to preach a sermon at St Paul's Cross urging the people to remain faithful to the truth as it was clearly set forth in the Scriptures. As a result, he was the first to be apprehended. Stripped of his ministry and placed under house arrest, he was confined for nearly a year.

But even this was not enough

for the cruel Bishop Bonner who had replaced Ridley as Bishop of London. Taken from his home, his wife and eleven young children, Rogers was confined in Newgate prison, a foul dump which he shared with thieves and murderers.

Prepare to die

On 22 January 1555 John Rogers was brought out of Newgate to face trial for his supposed heretical views. Prejudiced from first to last, the trial was a farce. The prisoner's answers made his opponents look foolish, but rather than address them they merely silenced him.

The main charges against him lay in his refusal to acknowledge any other except Jesus Christ as the head of the church — and his repudiation of the doctrine of 'transubstantiation', which stated that the sacramental bread and wine actually became the real body and blood of Christ. For these things this good man was condemned to die.

John Rogers had one request to make. He asked for an opportunity to speak once more to his wife, Adriana. Even this was refused. Perhaps he wished to tell Adriana where he had hidden the lengthy record he had made of his trial, and of the arguments he would have used had he been given opportunity. He well knew that if such a document were discovered it would be destroyed immediately.

On the morning of 4 February the jailer's wife hurried into the cell. 'Today you must prepare to die', she told Rogers. Already the pyre was being built. Again he begged one thing — that he might talk with his wife before he died. Again he was refused.

Led from Newgate to Smithfield, the condemned man was asked by one of the sheriffs who accompanied him whether he would now 'revoke his horrible doctrine'. 'That which I have preached I will seal with my blood', answered Rogers courageously.

The most piteous moment came as Rogers saw his wife with their ten young children, and one in her arms, waiting by the roadside to see him pass. Not even such a heart-rending sight could cause John Rogers to swerve from his stand on the unalterable truths of God's Word.

Marking out the way

Casting himself on the mercy of God in the words of Psalm 51, Rogers was chained to the stake. To the distressed onlookers, he appeared to be washing his hands in the leaping flames as they flared up around him. And so John Rogers joined that valiant host of men and women who have been faithful unto death.

When his family came to search the forlorn little cell after the brave man had died, one of his boys spotted a small black book half-hidden by the straw — it was that record of his trial that John Rogers had been so anxious to preserve! It had been saved for posterity despite all the craft of his persecutors.

John Rogers' unflinching courage inspired many another with fortitude, and especially his fellow martyrs called upon to follow the same fiery track to heaven — men such as John Bradford, Nicholas Ridley, Hugh Latimer and Thomas Cranmer.

In our own day, when all truth is regarded as relative rather than absolute, and when men and women of conviction are treated with growing intolerance, perhaps John Rogers can yet mark out the way for us. Like him, we must stand for the truth of the biblical gospel in a day marked by rampant ungodliness and false religion.

2. SORELY TESTED
CATHERINE BRANDON

Fourteen-year-old Catherine Willoughby was eagerly anticipating her marriage to eighteen-year-old Henry Brandon. Henry, only son of Sir Charles Brandon and Mary Rose (Henry VIII's favourite sister) was in direct line for the throne of England, second only to Henry VIII's daughter Mary.

Catherine, herself a wealthy heiress, was also descended from royalty. Born in 1519, she had lived with the Brandon family since the death of her father when she was only seven. As her guardian, Sir Charles had grown fond of Catherine and she fitted in happily with his three children — Henry and his sisters, Frances and Eleanor.

Then the unexpected happened. Shortly after the marriage of sixteen-year-old Frances to Henry Grey, Marquess of Dorset, the family was shocked by the untimely death of their mother, Mary Rose, at the early age of thirty-eight. A costly royal funeral followed which left Sir Charles acutely short of money, especially as he had already funded an expensive dowry for Frances.

Sir Charles Brandon and Mary Rose

Inner strength

A few months later, and to the astonishment of all, Sir Charles coolly announced that he had decided to marry Catherine himself. He was forty-eight and she only fourteen. Clearly he needed her fortune, the gossips whispered maliciously. His son, Henry, was so severely shocked at this turn of events that before long he became seriously ill. His father and Catherine had been married only a few months when the young man died.

We can only imagine Catherine's reaction to these things, but already the girl was beginning to know a source of inner and spiritual strength. These were the days when the great Reformation truths were being rediscovered and the circumstances of Catherine's life brought her into contact with the 'new religion' as it was dubbed. In 1517, two years before she was born, Martin Luther had nailed his ninety-five theses to the door of the Wittenberg church. Catherine loved those truths and would become a fearless advocate for them throughout life, regardless of the persecution that might follow.

Children

Catherine's first baby —ironically enough also named Henry Brandon — was born shortly after her fifteenth birthday. The following year a second boy, Charles, was born to the young mother. Glimpses of Sir Charles Brandon and his young wife appear in the chronicles of the times as they were present on many royal occasions. When the unfortunate Anne of Cleves, Henry VIII's rejected fourth wife, arrived in Rochester in 1540 they were among the welcoming party. And it was they who were entertaining the king when the infidelities of Catherine Howard — the King's capricious fifth wife, his 'rose without a thorn' — came to light.

But in 1545, when Catherine Brandon was still only twenty-six, her husband died at the age of sixty-two. Left with her two young sons, Henry aged eleven and his brother ten, Catherine poured all her affection on her boys. Conscientious and devoted as a mother, she taught them the principles of faith that had upheld her own life. The brothers joined the boy-king Edward VI in the royal schoolroom, and Henry became one of Edward's closest friends. Often Catherine's sons would visit Bradgate Park, for they were close in age to their niece, the precocious Lady Jane Grey, eldest daughter of Frances and Henry Grey. Both Henry and Charles grew into fine and capable young men.

At the royal court

After the death of Sir Charles, Catherine decided to join the royal court in London as one of the ladies-in-waiting of Henry's sixth wife, Katherine Parr, whom he had married in 1543. The fate of any of Henry's wives was precarious and particularly with the ruthless Bishop Stephen Gardiner, one of Henry's foremost advisers around the court. An inveterate opponent of evangelical truth, Gardiner did all in his power to crush the cause of true religion in the land. Great was his animosity when he learnt that the new Queen would gather her ladies-in-waiting around her to study the Scriptures. Bishop Hugh Latimer, already a close friend of Catherine Brandon, was often invited to preach to the royal ladies.

Known for her sharp wit, the new lady-in-waiting gained no favours from the pompous Gardiner — particularly when she decided to call her small poodle 'Gardiner'. He knew well that it was a joke at his expense, especially when the little dog sat obediently at her feet. But Gardiner was no poodle. He had helped to engineer the fearful torture and martyrdom of Anne Askew, another of the Queen's ladies-in-waiting whose unswerving support for the truths of Scripture cost her dearly.

Darkest moments

In 1551 came the supreme sorrow of Catherine's life. The 'sweating sickness' was stalking the land like a cruel predator. No one knew the cause of this dreaded disease, but hundreds of thousands fell victim to the all-consuming scourge. First came a blinding headache, followed by the profuse sweat that gave the condition its name. Death could come in a matter of hours. The young king Edward and his court were hastily evacuated to the country. Henry and Charles Brandon were both students at St John's College in Cambridge at the time; Henry was seventeen and his brother sixteen.

As soon as Catherine heard that the disease had reached Cambridge she immediately ordered her sons to her village home in Buckden not far away. But it was too late. By the time Catherine herself arrived, Henry was dead and Charles already unconscious. He died shortly after his brother. In one tragic hour Catherine had lost both her boys. The nation mourned the death of two of its brightest and most promising citizens.

How did the grieving mother's faith sustain her in those darkest moments? A letter has survived which she wrote to Sir William Cecil, later to be renowned as Lord Burleigh of Elizabeth's reign. A sentence or two from this letter gives us an insight into the depth of Catherine's understanding of the providence of God:

'I give God thanks, good Master Cecil, for all his benefits which it has pleased him to heap on me; and truly, I take this last (and to the first sight most sharp and bitter punishment) as not the least of his benefits. I have never been so well taught by any other before to know his power, his love and mercy and my own weakness'.

But in case this should sound too triumphalistic to our ears, Catherine goes on to confess that though she has received 'great comfort' from the Lord, and would much like to visit Sir William and his wife, she dared not trust herself to do so — in case her grief should overwhelm her and she should break down and weep in their presence.

Remarriage

Early in 1553, about two years after the death of her sons, Catherine Brandon remarried. Her new husband Sir Richard Bertie, a commoner and a staunch supporter of Protestant truths, was one who could give Catherine what she had always longed for — a secluded life away from the glare of court society. But only a few short months later, Edward VI's brief reign came to an end and the tragedy of Lady Jane Grey, Catherine's young relative still only fifteen, began to unfolded.

After Mary Tudor had claimed her father's throne, and Jane had courageously endured the executioner's axe, Catherine and Sir Richard knew that they too were marked out for destruction. For who should be released from prison and restored to power as Lord Chancellor under Mary, but Bishop Stephen Gardiner? Together with his co-persecutor, Bishop Edmund Bonner, he complied with Mary to stamp out the Protestant faith.

Hastily gathering a few belongings together and wrapping up her new baby Susan in a blanket, Catherine fled, sailing down the Thames on New Year's Day 1555. Sir Richard was waiting for her and together they took ship for the Netherlands. They had not gone far, however, before they were hopelessly lost in dense fog. After more near-disasters, the small family landed friendless in the Netherlands. Still afraid that Mary's agents might be on their track, they made their way on into Germany, arriving penniless in Wesel.

Destitute

Catherine, now thirty-six, and pregnant with her second child, was not used to such deprivations. Unable to speak German, the family was destitute indeed. At last they found shelter for the night in the porch of a church. But the God who cares for his people was watching over the fugitive family. The next day when Richard knocked at a nearby house to beg for shelter, he discovered that he was at the door of an English pastor, who kindly took them in.

After a brief respite they travelled on, now with the convenience of a covered wagon, their ultimate destination being Poland, then a Protestant state. Arriving there at last, King Sigismund welcomed the family and before long a son was born to Catherine whom the couple called Peregrine — for this infant was a child of their homelessness and peregrinations. For the next four years Catherine and Richard remained in Poland, even helping their benefactor to govern the province of Lithuania.

At last in 1558 came the welcome news that Bloody Mary, responsible for almost three hundred appalling martyrdoms, was dead and Elizabeth was on the throne. The exiles returned to England and during her remaining twenty-one years of life, Catherine agitated constantly for a fuller reformation of the church. Elizabeth's compromises troubled and distressed her. Catherine could well be entitled to the honour of being called one of the first Puritan women.

A sentence from another letter to Sir William Cecil sums up Catherine's trust and devotion to the God whom she had revered from childhood: 'God... works all the best to them that love and fear him. Were not this hope of him thoroughly settled in me, I think my very heart would burst for sorrow'.

3. Steadfast in zeal

Edward VI

The birth of a royal baby is usually an occasion for great celebrations among the English — and no birth was more so than that of Edward Tudor, long awaited son of Henry VIII. Cannons from the Tower of London thundered over two thousand salutes to welcome his birth, while bells peeled out across the city and bonfires lit up the night sky.

Born on 12 October 1537, Prince Edward was the son of Henry's third wife, Jane Seymour. But despite the celebrations, the child had an unhappy start to life. When he was only twelve days old his mother died unexpectedly of complications arising from the birth.

Henry's grief turned to frenetic anxiety over his infant son's health. Smothered in shawls to prevent any draughts reaching him, Edward spent his early months in a purpose-built nursery at Hampton Court. His rooms were scrubbed and swept twice daily, all his food was tested by others to prevent poisoning, and no visitors were allowed near the babe.

Hampton Court

Family life

Although Edward was a cheerful youngster, one thing was missing — the motherless prince knew little true affection. All was soon to change, however, with his father's final marriage to Katherine Parr in 1543. At last the six-year-old experienced some family life, as Katherine insisted that Edward and his half-sister Elizabeth should spend more time with their father. Edward's response to his stepmother's affection was immediate and strong. More than this, Katherine arranged for boys of Edward's own age, sons of the nobility, to join him in his schoolroom.

As the prince's education began in earnest, we see God's overruling hand both for Edward and for the future of the Christian church in England. Henry VIII had vacillated between Roman Catholicism and the doctrines of the Reformation for the best part of his reign, persecuting the adherents of first one and then the other. A pragmatist to the last, he decided that the Tudor posterity would best be served by a Reformed upbringing for his son.

Achievement

Richard Cox and John Cheke were appointed to be the boy's tutors. Both were well-known friends of the Reformation — the movement that was rapidly restoring the Bible and the great doctrine of justification by faith alone to the heart of the Christian religion after centuries of neglect.

It is evident that Edward was an exceptionally able child. By the time he was seven he was reading Latin texts fluently, and soon French and Greek were added to his timetable. A weighty tome of his childhood writings has survived, containing fifty or more lengthy Latin essays and as many in Greek. A school

report (had there been such a
thing at the time) would have
complimented the prince
on all-round achievement.
However, we are told that
the Tudor bottom was
smacked on occasions when
young Edward grew tired
of memorising the book of
Proverbs in Latin! Later a
'whipping boy' stood in for
the prince, though doubtless
Edward was obliged to watch
as another received the
chastisement he deserved.

At nine years of age the
prince undertook his first
royal responsibilities, welcoming the Admiral of France as he
arrived on a state visit. Three brief months later, the weight of
kingship fell on the child's shoulders when his father died in
January 1547.

The boy-king

Then came the elaborate ceremony of coronation. The boy-king
— clad in a gown of crimson velvet embroidered with gold and a
cape of white velvet decorated with rubies and diamonds — was
escorted from the Tower of London to Westminster Abbey riding
a horse draped in crimson.

A long and tedious ceremony followed and Edward was
allowed short rests during that auspicious day. The crown was
too heavy for a nine-year-old head and (recording his memories

in his personal journal) Edward commented dolefully that he was obliged to wear it throughout a banquet that followed the ceremonies. He crept into his bed that night a weary child.

Effective rule of the country during Edward's minority was entrusted to a Council of Regency comprising sixteen men. Edward Seymour, the prince's uncle, was in overall charge with the younger of his two uncles, Thomas Seymour, also in a prominent position.

When Thomas Seymour married the boy's stepmother, Katherine Parr, Edward was not above playing off one uncle against the other, particularly if he needed extra pocket money! But Edward soon detected the underhand motives behind his younger uncle's actions, all designed to snatch power for himself.

Evangelical convictions

Before he died Henry VIII had done more for the progress of true religion in England than he ever intended. By surrounding his young son with men of evangelical principles, he had created a circumstance which God would mightily use. Before long it became evident from Edward's own writings that his personal sympathies lay with the Bible-based teaching of the Reformation. Later these same truths became his own deeply held beliefs.

One person whose influence seems to have been crucial to the boy's understanding was his French master Jean Belmain. Edward's French essays reveal the intensity of the boy's evangelical convictions — an intensity which Belmain tried to modify in case it became a source of political embarrassment. Edward loved to hear sermons and made detailed notes of addresses by preachers such as Bishop Nicholas Ridley. Sadly, his notebook has not survived.

As he grew older the young king began to use his authority to back reformations in the church, and the gospel in England progressed at an astonishing pace. In 1552 Archbishop Cranmer's revised Book of Common Prayer came into use, but all this was still not fast enough for Edward. When John Hooper was about to be consecrated as Bishop of Gloucester, he learned that the service book required him to wear certain vestments and take an oath in the name of the saints. He objected strongly. Such ideas, he maintained, were unbiblical. Who should come to his rescue but the thirteen-year-old king?

'Are these offices ordained in the name of saints or of God?' he enquired imperiously, and with one stroke of his pen slashed through the offending words in the prayer book service. Edward was clearly a Tudor monarch in the making.

Threat of war

A yet more notable scene took place shortly after this — a high profile dispute of predictable tension between the young king and his half-sister Mary, now in her thirties. Mary, a devout Roman Catholic, wished to celebrate mass in private. She wept and begged her young brother to give permission for her priests to conduct such services. Edward also wept, for he was fond of Mary, but he remained adamant. Mary departed insisting that she would emigrate rather than comply with such laws.

However, Mary's closeness to her cousin Charles V, now Holy Roman Emperor, compounded the situation. To offend Mary could have serious political consequences for the country.

Not surprisingly the Emperor's anger was unleashed and he instructed his ambassador to threaten war against England.

Edward's councillors arrived. On their knees these anxious men urged the gravity of the situation and begged Edward to compromise. Only when the boy threatened to burst into tears once more did they retire defeated. War did not follow, only a dramatic but unsuccessful rescue attempt to remove Mary from the country.

Succession

In February 1553, Edward, still only fifteen years of age, but now taking an active part in government, caught measles. He made some initial recovery, but began to undertake royal duties again before he had regained full health. As spring turned to summer a harsh dry cough and burning fever developed. Soon it became clear that he was seriously ill. His doctor privately diagnosed tuberculosis, but publicly suggested more rest. As the year progressed Edward was having difficulties eating and sleeping: he was clearly dying.

One thing troubled him above all else. He knew that under his father's will the crown would pass to his half-sister, Mary. He greatly feared that if Mary succeeded to the throne the progress of true Christianity in England, for which his short life had been lived, would be halted or even reversed.

Other politicians also knew that they would lose their heads if Mary became queen. The only answer, therefore, seemed to be to change the succession. Some have said that the sick boy was manipulated, but once his chief advisor the Duke of Northumberland had made the initial suggestion, the dying king was determined on such a course of action. He would leave his throne to his fifteen-year-old cousin, Lady Jane Grey, an earnest

Christian girl and in any case next in line for the crown after his half-sisters, Mary and Elizabeth.

When lawyers were summoned to effect the change in Henry VIII's will, they naturally hesitated. Not until Edward demanded imperiously that they comply was it officially altered in favour of Lady Jane.

Dying prayer

Now Edward was at peace. Turning to the wall he began to pray:

'Lord God, deliver me out of this miserable and wretched life, and take me among thy chosen: howbeit, not my will but thy will be done. Lord, I commit my spirit to thee. O Lord! Thou knowest how happy it were for me to be with thee: yet for thy chosen's sake, send me life and health, that I may truly serve thee.

'O Lord my God, bless thy people. O Lord God save thy chosen people of England! O my God defend this realm ... and maintain thy true religion, that I and my people may praise thy holy name, for thy Son Jesus Christ's sake'.

Then Edward became conscious that he was not alone; his doctor was standing nearby. 'I thought you were farther away', he said. 'We heard you talking to yourself', the doctor responded. 'I was praying', replied Edward simply.

Three hours later Edward spoke his last words: 'I am faint. Lord have mercy upon me and take my spirit'. On 6 July 1553 the zealous and able young king, whose evangelical convictions never wavered, died. A fearsome thunderstorm broke out over London on that day — perhaps a gloomy portent of the days of trouble that lay ahead for the true church of God in England.

For despite Edward's attempt to change the succession, Mary raised an army, the country flocked to her banner and quickly defeated troops loyal to Lady Jane. And by 19 July 1553 Mary Tudor was proclaimed Queen of England, and began her reign. In February the following year Lady Jane and her young husband were executed, and Mary's reign of persecution and death began as she determined to stamp out the work of the Reformation in her country. But despite it all, Edward VI's reign had left an indelible stamp on the religious life of England.

4. DYING WELL

JOHN BUNYAN

The sky was dark and threatening as John Bunyan mounted his horse that August morning in 1688. It had been an errand of compassion that had brought him to Reading — a long detour in his journey from Bedford to London. But now, grateful to God that he had managed to effect the reconciliation between a father and son that he had hoped to accomplish there, he set off for London.

Despite the gathering storm he was anxious to keep his engagement to preach in Whitechapel and not disappoint the congregation that had so long anticipated his visit. Recently recovered from a debilitating illness, Bunyan rode at a steady pace. But the skies grew blacker still and it was not long before a violent storm broke upon him. Both horse and rider were soon drenched by the torrential rain, while the roads, never much better than rubble-filled ditches, quickly turned to mud tracks. There was no alternative for Bunyan, however, but to struggle onwards towards London.

Celestial city

Soaked through and exhausted, Bunyan at last reached the home of John Strudwick who owned a chemist shop in Snow Hill, Holborn. Here he was welcomed with concern and kindness as his friends did their best to care for the well-loved preacher, now evidently feverish and suffering from his exposure to the elements. After a day or two of rest John Bunyan — renowned author of The Pilgrim's Progress — appeared his genial self once more and was eager to preach as he had promised, despite earnest appeals from his friends against taking such a risk.

This initial recovery, however, had hidden the seriousness of Bunyan's condition and not long after he had preached, the full effects of that ride became apparent. His health deteriorated rapidly and soon pneumonia set in. Those who watched over him could see that John Bunyan's own pilgrimage was swiftly drawing to a close. A mere ten days later, and before his wife Elizabeth could be summoned, the 'Immortal Dreamer' had crossed the bridgeless River into the Celestial City.

I go to the Father

The 'last enemy' had sprung unawares on John Bunyan at the comparatively early age of sixty but the enemy gained no advantage by his sudden attack. Here was one of Christ's faithful servants, well prepared against his assaults. 'Weep not for me but for yourselves', he whispered as the end drew near and he could see the obvious distress of those who watched around him. Like many other Christians as they face death, Bunyan's thoughts were clearly turning to that solid foundation of his faith laid in the atoning sacrifice of his Saviour. 'I go to the Father of our Lord Jesus Christ, who will, no doubt through the mediation of his blessed Son, receive me, though a sinner; where I hope we ere long shall meet and sing the new song and remain everlastingly happy, world without end'. These words, spoken with much difficulty but in confidence and hope, were his last.

Sometimes when we read accounts like this we are troubled about how we ourselves will cope with death. We fear lest by weakness or lack of faith we may fail the Lord at the last. Is there any way, we may ask, to prepare ourselves while strength and health are still ours? It would seem from his writings that Bunyan himself had learnt lessons long years before that August day in 1688, lessons which came to his aid in his time of need.

Sentence of death

Bunyan's life spanned tempestuous years for the church of Jesus Christ. Born in 1628, three years after Charles I had ascended the throne — and dying the year of the 'Glorious Revolution' when religious toleration was granted at last — he faced many years of suffering for Christ's sake. Apart from the period of Cromwell's Protectorate, they were times when crippling fines, confiscation of goods, banishment, imprisonment and even death had been the order of the day for many faithful Christians who would not compromise their spiritual principles.

Bunyan himself had spent the twelve best years of his manhood in Bedford county jail. As he faced those bleak circumstances, he wrote, 'I was made to see that if ever I would suffer rightly, I must first pass a sentence of death upon everything that can properly be called a thing of this life, even to reckon myself, my wife, my children, my health, my enjoyment and all, as dead to me and myself as dead to them'. Like everyone else, Bunyan rejoiced in these legitimate pleasures of life, yet he had learnt to hold them with a light grasp. But such a 'sentence of death' did not leave an emotional vacuum for Bunyan, for (he continued) he had learnt instead 'to live on God that is invisible'.

In November 1660 when he faced his first imprisonment he was indeed called to pass such a 'sentence of death' on his dearest joys — Mary, his blind daughter and eldest of his four children, was only ten at the time. Writing of these circumstances Bunyan says, 'The parting with my wife and poor children hath oft been to me as the pulling of my flesh from my bones ... the hardships and miseries that my poor family was like to meet with ... especially my poor blind child who lay nearest my heart than all I had besides ... would break my heart in pieces.

'I was as a man pulling down his house upon the head of his wife and children; yet thought I, I must do it, I must do it'. Love for Christ and faithfulness to his truth had made it a necessity.

Crossing the river

Those hard lessons had trained Bunyan to view the things of time from the perspective of eternity. He had long learnt to look upon death itself, that king of terrors, with a steady eye. In his great allegory, *The Pilgrim's progress*, he accompanied each of his pilgrims one by one to the brink of the River of Death. Mr Valiant-for-Truth passed courageously through the dark waters calling out, 'Death, where is thy sting? Grave, where is thy victory?' and Bunyan heard all the trumpets sounding for him on the other side.

The waters were deep indeed and overflowed their banks as old Mr Honest crossed over, but Good Conscience lent him a hand and so crying out, 'Grace reigns!' he too arrived safely on firm ground. Mr Ready-to-Halt threw away his crutches and entered the river exclaiming, 'Welcome life', while Mr Despondency, in spite of many fears, entered the cold waters saying, 'Farewell night, welcome day!' His daughter, who shared his fearful spirit, was heard singing as she passed through, though none could catch the words of her song.

Mr Standfast, that noble and prayerful pilgrim, found the river unusually calm when he crossed over; but not all of Bunyan's pilgrims had so easy a passage. Christian himself struggled as he entered the river and in his dream Bunyan heard him call out to his companion Hopeful, 'I sink in deep waters; the billows go over my head'. The sins of his past life rose up to distress him and rob him of any confidence that he would ever gain the farther shore.

But Hopeful was near at hand to hold him up and point him away from his failures to the mercy of God. Perhaps words spoken by one of the Shining Ones before he entered the River came back to his mind: 'You shall find it [the River] deeper or shallower as you trust in the King of the Place'; for as Christian was grappling with the turbulent waves he suddenly cried out, 'Oh, I see him again! And he tells me, "When thou passest through the waters I will be with thee, and through the rivers, they shall not overflow thee".'

The glories of heaven

So it was that, through the experiences of his pilgrims, Bunyan had thought often about death, and in this way prepared himself for the time when he too would reach the end of the journey. But the glories of heaven were also frequently in his mind. Life was insecure for the followers of Christ, and the certainty of the joys awaiting Christ's believing people encouraged and gladdened his heart.

During his first period of imprisonment Bunyan wrote a treatise called *The Holy City*. Lifting his eyes from the sordid surroundings of his cheerless prison, he roamed in imagination along the streets and through the palaces of the New Jerusalem. Little wonder that he longed to be there! In his work *The desire of the Righteous granted* we can almost catch the passion of his heart as he writes, 'To see Christ then, to see him as he is in glory is a sight worth going from relations and out of the body and through the jaws of death to see … to see him preparing mansion houses for those his poor ones that are now by his enemies kicked to and fro like footballs in the world; and is not this a blessed sight?'

Perhaps the finest description of heaven outside the pages of Scripture comes from Bunyan's pen and is found at the end of the *Pilgrim's progress*. It needs to be read in full to gain any true appreciation of the magnitude and glory of the Celestial City, as it appeared to the eyes of John Bunyan as he looked in through the gates.

And so as he lay dying, far from his wife Elizabeth and from his home, we are not surprised that he could exclaim, 'O! who is able to conceive the inexpressible, inconceivable joys that are there? None but those who have tasted of them'.

5. LABOUR NOT IN VAIN

HANS EGEDE

Hans Egede was absorbed in a book. Scarcely could he raise his eyes from its pages. Meals and sleep were forgotten as he roamed in imagination through the wild wastes of a strange and beautiful land, following the steps of the Viking explorer, Eric the Red. With a sigh he at last closed *The saga of Eric the Red* for he had reached the final page of his tale. Crossing to the window, Hans Egede gazed westward, wandering in thought among the frozen shimmering heights of that unknown country Eric had called Green Land.

Born in Harstad, northern Norway in 1686, Hans Egede had studied theology in Copenhagen and at the age of twenty-one was appointed pastor of a small Lutheran church. The village of Vaagen, a tiny dot on the world map in the Lofoten Islands, lies far to the north west of Norway, and here Hans diligently served his people. Sunday by Sunday he preached to this rugged fishing community whose men folk daily ventured into the turbulent waters of the Norwegian Sea in their small fishing vessels. He loved his people and they responded warmly to him in return. And not many months passed before Hans won the affections of a local girl, Gertrud Rask — who proved a fine, unselfish wife to the young pastor.

Eric the Red

But now Hans could not banish from his mind the heroic adventures of the Viking explorer. Three hundred years earlier, so the story ran, Eric the Red (named for his flaming red hair and beard and perhaps his temper) was exiled for three years from his Iceland home on charges of manslaughter. Where could he go? Then he recalled that half a century earlier a Norwegian explorer had claimed to have sighted a new land far to the west of Iceland. Eric decided that this was his opportunity to find that land. After sailing for five hundred miles he came at last to a frozen wasteland. But rounding the tip of the northern hemisphere's largest island, Eric discovered a pleasant habitable area on the west of this new country. Here he decided to settle and live out his exile.

On his return to Iceland, Eric claimed to have discovered a pleasant fruitful land — which he called Green Land to make it sound more appealing than Ice Land. Setting sail once more in the year 985, he took twenty-five ships of hopeful colonists with him, although eleven ships either sank or turned back. Eric the Red spent the rest of his life exploring and colonising Greenland, and it is said that his son Lief, a Christian man, set up the first church in Greenland. Soon a colony 3000 strong was built up, but an epidemic of smallpox in the year 1002 virtually wiped out the whole community.

No one knew what had happened since to the surviving colonists. Were any Christians left in Greenland? Egede wondered. The thought of their need preyed on Hans Egede's mind and burdened him night and day. Even his people began to notice that strange faraway look in their pastor's eyes. At last Hans could bear the strain no longer. He told Gertrud that he must go to Greenland and discover what had happened and preach the gospel of Christ to the people once more.

Hazardous journey

To his grief, Gertrud said, 'No'. She could not face the thought of uprooting from her Vaagan home and travelling to who-knows-where in search of unknown Christians. But gradually she could see that the weight of concern was destroying her husband. At last she agreed to go; but many long years would pass before Hans and Gertrud could realise their objective. No company would risk providing ships, nor would anyone offer support. But never one to be denied, Hans Egede agitated ceaselessly, with the vision of those needy Christians ever before him.

At last in 1721 Egede's prayer and persistence won the day. The Danish king provided three ships and a salary for the would-be missionary. But if Hans thought his problems were over when the small party set sail from Bergen, he was mistaken. The journey was hazardous, and one of the three boats foundered in the icy waters. What did Hans expect when at last he arrived? Far from discovering the 'green land' of Eric the Red's exaggerated and glowing description, he discovered an icy treeless wilderness.

Sailing on round Cape Farewell at the tip of the island, the situation seemed more hopeful when he came to the deep and beautiful Eriksfjord and finally went ashore. But where were the descendants of those first Christians? As suspicious Inuit people gathered around the newcomers, Hans soon 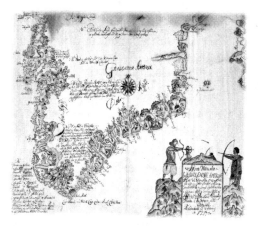 realised that these people knew nothing of any such settlement, nor of any Christian gospel. Three hundred years had passed since the last of the Viking colonists had died out. If Hans Egede

wished to bring the Christian message to the hardy Arctic peoples
he would have to start again right from the beginning.

Impervious to the gospel

Many were the hardships Hans and Gertrud faced. First there
was the language barrier. Slowly and painstakingly Hans began
to learn the Inuit (Eskimo) tongue. But still the people seemed
unable to take in the basic concepts of the truths that burned
in Egede's heart. Where no light of the Christian gospel has
penetrated for countless generations, crude and evil habits master
a people. The priests, or Angekoks as they were called, quickly
saw Hans Egede and the message he taught as a threat to their
way of life. Murderous plots were often afoot, and only the hand
of God saved the missionary and his family from a violent end.

For many months of the year the Greenland sun never rises and
the gloom of a continual night shrouds the land. As temperatures
plummeted during those long winter days, it seemed that Hans,
Gertrud and their children might well starve to death for they were
not skilled hunters like the Inuit people. Sometimes even water
put on the coals to boil would freeze before the fire generated
sufficient heat to raise the temperature. But the greatest chill
was the one that rested on the hearts of the people. They seemed
impervious to the earnest pleadings of the ardent evangelist.

Small church

When a smallpox epidemic decimated the population, Egede was
obliged to move further north, founding a small colony which
he named Godthåb (now called Nuuk, capital of Greenland).
And slowly, very slowly, he began to see some improvement
in the attitudes and habits of the people among whom he lived.

Realising their basic need of teaching, Egede translated Luther's *Small Catechism* into the Inuit language and began work on the New Testament. And still he looked and prayed for conversions and spiritual fruit for his labours.

After some years a small church was built and in 1733, when Hans had been in Greenland for twelve years, the first missionaries from Count Zinzendorf's brave Moravian settlement arrived to strengthen Egede's lonely witness. But two years later another devastating epidemic of smallpox swept through the community. One dark December day in 1734 Gertrud herself, his courageous wife, succumbed to the illness and died. Heartbroken, Hans found this trial more than his forlorn spirit could bear. He laid his wife's body in a coffin, but could not bring himself to bury it. Rather, like the Israelites of old who carried Joseph's remains back with them to the promised land, he too would take Gertrud home one day.

Left with four children, through the dreary months of the Arctic winter, the pioneer missionary found a deep black depression settling on his spirit. He seemed unable to face the hardships without Gertrud. And before long he decided he could stay no longer. In August 1735, eight months after Gertrud had died, he preached his final sermon to the small gathering of Inuit Christians. The verse he chose was a sad one indeed: 'I have laboured in vain, I have spent my strength for nothing' (Isaiah 49:4).

Amazing change

Leaving his oldest son, Paul, behind, Hans Egede took his second son Neils, his two small daughters and the coffin carrying the remains of his faithful wife, and set sail for Copenhagen. Had all that suffering, all the prayers, tears and sacrifice really been in vain? Certainly not! Perhaps Hans had forgotten the second half of his text which says, 'Yet surely my just reward is with the Lord, and my work with my God'. Though seed may lie dormant for long years the promise of God is that one day it will yield a plentiful harvest.

Gradually Hans Egede recovered something of his old spirit, and realised that he could still serve his struggling converts in Godthåb. First he gathered resources to finance projects to aid the work. Then he established a school to train other missionaries to labour in that difficult field. And lastly he completed his translation of the New Testament into the Inuit language.

When Hans Egede's second son Neils returned to Greenland, determined to carry on his father's work, he discovered an amazing change had taken place. The fruit of that long-delayed harvest was beginning to be gathered in. He found that the name 'Egede' was revered among the Inuit people. 'He was more than our father', they declared simply. Neils established another colony further north, calling it Egedeminde ('in memory of Egede') — a name which still appears on modern maps alongside its Inuit counterpart.

Called 'the Apostle of Greenland', Hans Egede died in Copenhagen in 1758. His labours were 'not in vain in the Lord' and only eternity will show the extent of blessing still resulting from them. And it may be that some unknown servant of the Lord today, working in trying and unpromising circumstances, will likewise be vindicated in years to come.

6. Changed by grace

Selina, Countess of Huntingdon

'Were you named after the great Selina, Countess of Huntingdon?'
I recently asked a young Christian woman, who was also named
Selina. But like so many today she had not heard of any 'great'
Selina. Who then was Selina, Countess of Huntingdon?

Born in Northamptonshire in 1707, into a family that could
trace its ancestry back to royalty, Selina was the second of
Washington Shirley's three daughters. But her childhood was far
from happy and her home was a place of bitterness and acrimony.
Her parents split up when Selina was only six. Her mother
moved to France taking her youngest daughter with her. Family
wrangling over property further marred her childhood, and not
until she married Theophilus Hastings, Earl of Huntingdon,
when she was twenty-one years of age did she know any settled
home life.

Although the Shirley family was both prosperous and
influential, the Hastings family was more so, owning property
in Yorkshire, Leicestershire and Northamptonshire. The young
couple regularly mingled with royalty and it was Theophilus
who carried the Sword of State at the coronation of George II.

Forceful

With a natural flair for organisation, Selina managed her
husband's estates. Four sons and two daughters were born to
the couple in quick succession. But childbirth carried high risks
in the eighteenth century, and Selina suffered from constant ill-
health. The remedies of purges and vomitings that her thirty-two-

stone doctor proposed did little to improve either her condition or her spirits.

Quick-tempered and forceful by disposition, Selina was also sensitive and conscientious, and did all in her power to improve the lot of those who farmed the Hastings lands or worked at her Leicestershire home, Donington Hall. The young Countess possessed all that money could buy, but she was a dissatisfied woman. Religious and generous though she was, her mind was restless and troubled. Her hasty temper often got the better of her. 'I would undergo everything to come to a true knowledge of my Saviour', she confessed to her sister-in-law, Lady Betty Hastings. So despairing did she become that friends of Theophilus advised him to have her put into a mental asylum — a thing he would never do.

Guilt removed

But when her other three sisters-in-law (Margaret, Anne and Frances Hastings) were deeply influenced by the preaching of Yorkshire evangelist Benjamin Ingham, a friend of John Wesley, Selina too was profoundly affected. 'Since I have known the Lord Jesus Christ for salvation, I have been as happy as an angel', announced Margaret Hastings artlessly. This was a dimension of religion entirely new to the Countess of Huntingdon.

All her life Selina had feared death but in July 1739 its reality came very close as she faced a period of serious illness. She thought of her husband and her young family, but mostly she thought of her spiritual condition. Then Margaret's words flashed vividly before her mind again: 'Since I have known the Lord Jesus Christ for salvation I have been as happy as an angel'. From her bed Selina lifted up her heart to the Saviour with the earnest prayer that she too might know the inner happiness through

Christ that her sister-in-law had found.

God heard her cry and immediately all her distress and fears were removed. At peace spiritually, Selina's physical condition began to improve. As soon as she was able she wrote to her sisters-in-law to share the joy she now experienced in the knowledge that her guilt was removed and sins forgiven. The change was immediate and obvious. Even her maid noted that her mistress had not fallen into a rage for many months.

Social suicide

Never half-hearted in anything she did, Selina began to align herself with such despised Methodists as Benjamin Ingham, knowing that this would set every tongue in court wagging. To her friends this was social suicide and some of them begged Theophilus to see if he could moderate his wife's religious enthusiasm. Sending for his old Oxford tutor and friend, Martin Benson, now Bishop of Gloucester, Theophilus arranged for a discussion to take place between Benson and Selina. Much of the conversation centred round the rights and wrongs of the new field preachers — men such as the Wesley brothers, Ingham and especially George Whitefield whom Benson himself had just ordained in 1739.

Quite clearly Benson found himself out-manoeuvred by the young woman in front of him. 'She plainly and faithfully urged upon him the awful responsibility of his station under that great head of the Church, Jesus Christ', we read. This was more than the bishop could stand. Jumping up, he hurried to make his departure. But before he left he said with a measure of chagrin that he regretted the day he had ever ordained George Whitefield, for he recognised that the change in the Countess was directly due to the new preaching associated with the young preacher's name. But Selina had the last word. 'My Lord', she said, 'mark my words, when you come upon your dying bed, that will be one of the few ordinations you will reflect upon with complacence' — a prediction that came true.

Sadness

Selina's family life was tinged with sadness. Two of her sons, Ferdinando and George, aged eleven and thirteen, died of smallpox within an eight-month period. But the grief that nearly broke Selina's spirit was the loss of her husband Theophilus in 1746. Their love had been strong and deep. He died of a stroke, unexpectedly and alone, in his home in Downing Street, leaving Selina a widow at only thirty-nine. As she grieved near his grave in Ashby-de-la-Zouch, she might be excused for thinking that all purpose in her life had gone for ever. In fact it had only begun.

During the early years of her Christian experience, the Countess relied heavily on the help she received from Charles and John Wesley. In return she encouraged them in every way, doing all in her power to promote their labours. But after the death of Theophilus, her friendship with Howell Harris and Philip Doddridge, coupled with her lack of a strong assurance of faith, gradually led her ever closer to the doctrines held by the Calvinistic Methodists. When George Whitefield, who had spent the last four years in America, arrived home in July 1748, Selina asked him to call on her as soon as he could.

Personal chaplain

Selina now spent part of her time in her fashionable home in the one-time village of Chelsea, on the banks of the Thames. There she planned to invite members of parliament, the aristocracy, and even royalty to her drawing room, to hear the preaching of Whitefield or occasionally of Wesley and others. To accomplish this purpose she appointed Whitefield as her personal chaplain — a privilege she enjoyed as a peeress of the realm. Many of the nobility accepted her invitations — few could resist her charm and strength of personality — and came under the searching and powerful preaching of Whitefield. Among them were her aunt, the lovely Lady Fanny Shirley, mistress of Lord Chesterfield; Chesterfield himself and his long-suffering wife; the atheistic Lord Bolingbroke and his half brother Lord St John; and numerous others reckoned among the celebrities of the day. All could be found at Selina's drawing-room meetings.

Acceptance

As the Countess requested in her will that no biography should be written of her, none was attempted until almost ninety years after these events had taken place. As a result, many of those converted or influenced by these gatherings of the nobility were forgotten with the passage of time. Among the most significant, however, were Lady Fanny Shirley, Lord St John and Lord Dartmouth — later to become Colonial Secretary, President of the Board of Trade and President of the Royal Society. Even the Prince of Wales who died in 1752 was much affected. By her patronage the Countess nursed and protected the fledgling Methodist movement and gained for the Christian gospel a degree of acceptance in high places, where only apathy and antagonism had existed before.

Luke Tyerman, one of Whitefield's earliest biographers, sums up this period in the Countess's life and evaluates its effect in these words: 'The gatherings in Chelsea were profoundly interesting spectacles; and never till the Day of Judgement will it be ascertained to what extent the preaching of the youthful Whitefield affected the policy of some of England's greatest statesmen and moulded the character of some of England's highest aristocratic families'.

With an unquenchable zeal for the conversion of the men and women of her generation, Selina, now in her early forties, stood poised for a life of extraordinary usefulness in the kingdom of God.

7. HAVING COMPASSION

SELINA, COUNTESS OF HUNTINGDON

As the horse-drawn carriage bumped along the uneven roads between London and the south coast, the Countess of Huntingdon must have wondered many times whether her journey would prove worthwhile. Selina's youngest son Henry, not yet seventeen, was suffering from an uncommon condition that was not only robbing him of his eyesight but had become life-threatening. Desperate for a remedy, she was bringing him to the fishing village of Brighthelmstone — now called Brighton — to see if sea bathing would help.

How surprised must the Countess have been when a stranger stopped her in the street saying, 'Oh Madam, you are come!' 'What do you know of me?' asked Selina in surprise. 'Madam, I saw you in a dream three years ago, dressed as you are now', answered the woman. She then proceeded to tell of a dream she could never forget in which she had seen a tall woman dressed just like Selina. She had understood that when this woman came to Brighthelmstone she would be the means of doing much good.

With such an introduction, it was not long before Selina was able to draw together a small group of women and teach them regularly from the Scriptures. Unknown to the Countess, Henry's illness and subsequent death at the age of eighteen, was to prove a gateway into her lifework. Conversions among this group of women would lead to many more conversions in the town.

Chapels

This was in 1757, and by 1759 there were so many seeking

regular gospel preaching that the need to build a chapel in Brighton became imperative. Much of Selina's money was tied up in property but by borrowing from a friend and selling some of her jewels the Countess raised £1200 and erected 'a small but neat chapel', opened in 1761. Later that same year she opened another chapel ten miles inland, using the great hall of an old mansion.

Soon she cast her eyes further afield and conceived the bold plan of building in Bath, playground of the rich and indolent, where the aristocracy repaired to 'take the waters'. Here she would provide an attractive meeting place where evangelical preachers could address the people. As a loyal member of the Church of England, Selina ensured that no service conducted in her chapels clashed with regular parish services. They were intended to supplement rather than replace them.

Training preachers

When Lord Chesterfield, arrogant, sociable and amoral, saw the elegant windows and turrets of the Countess' new chapel in Bath taking shape, an idea struck him. As his country mansion, Bretby Hall in Derbyshire was little used, he decided to offer her the loan of it. The Countess accepted the proposal and soon a flourishing gospel cause was established in Derbyshire. Back in Sussex another chapel was opened in Lewes in 1765.

All this chapel building threw up another problem. How could she fill the pulpits? Many of her friends rallied to her cause and were willing to travel the country at her behest — William Romaine, John Berridge, Howell Harris, Henry Venn, John Fletcher and others filled her pulpits in rotation. The Countess acted as a modern-day church secretary, but not just for one church. She had half a dozen or more pulpits to fill, and still the requests came in for more chapels and more preachers. Selina's influence had steadily increased through the years, her main aim being to promote a reformation of the ministry of the Church of England.

Copthorne Chapel West Sussex

To do this she tried to lobby the bishops until they agreed to ordain men with evangelical convictions. But if the bishops refused to ordain such men, there was only one answer — the Methodists must train their own preachers!

Demanding project

Consulting with Howell Harris, who lived at Trevecca in Breconshire, Selina discovered he had long had the same vision. Together they planned the details and Trevecca College was born. An old farmhouse, situated not 500 yards from Harris's farming community, could be transformed into suitable accommodation for students. Now turned sixty years of age and suffering indifferent health, the Countess was embarking on the most demanding project of her life. The prospective college would have to be furnished, books provided, tutors engaged and, most important of all, suitable students recruited. In August 1768, on her sixty-first birthday, Trevecca College was opened. Each year as the anniversary of the opening came around there would be memorable gatherings at Trevecca as thousands came together for days of special preaching.

Division

The years immediately following the opening of Trevecca, 1770-1771, were to prove Selina's hardest. Tensions between John Wesley and the Countess, whom John Berridge laughingly called 'Pope John and Pope Joan', had been building up, especially since the opening of the college. During his annual conference in August 1770, Wesley had spoken out strongly against empty religious professions. But in his published Minutes of the conference he expressed himself in a most unfortunate manner, and to any candid reader seemed to be suggesting that good works were essential for salvation. This struck at the heart of the great Reformation doctrine of justification by faith alone. The Countess wept openly when she read the Minutes and was convinced that her old friend had reneged on the faith. She immediately banned Wesley from her pulpits.

Although a degree of understanding was re-established the following year, the damage was done. A literary war broke out, with good men hurling insults at each other through the medium of the printed page. A sorry spectacle, it brought about a permanent division in the evangelical revival.

Tireless zeal

From this time onwards the Countess gave herself unremittingly to the care of her students and the establishment of chapels. During the 1770s they sprung up like mushrooms in all parts of the country, their pulpits supplied by Trevecca students.

The Countess herself planned the students' itineraries, arranged their accommodation, clothed them, provided them with horses and even pocket money for the journey — all at her own expense. Insisting on the highest standards, she could often be dictatorial, particularly with those who were not prepared to go where she sent them. But they knew she loved them and confided freely in her.

Selina in turn followed them with numerous letters and prayed earnestly for them. During her lifetime at least 250 young men received a basic training at Trevecca — a training they would never have received under normal circumstances. Some of them were numbered among the most outstanding preachers of the late eighteenth century.

Broad Oak Chapel Canterbury Kent

Wherever men and women were to be found, there the Countess longed to plant a chapel. Nor did her vision end in her own land. When George Whitefield bequeathed Bethesda Orphanage to her at his death in 1770, she gathered together a group of students willing to go to Georgia to take up the work. A serious fire in 1773 destroyed much of the premises and the American War of Independence put a final end to the project, but she still yearned to reach the Indians of America with the gospel of Christ. At the age of seventy she was even prepared to undertake the hazardous journey across the Atlantic herself, if only to make garments for Indian children! To Belgium, Spain, France and even the South Sea Islands she planned to send missionaries.

Of course she made mistakes and there were failures, but no one grieved over these more than the Countess herself. Above all it is her tireless zeal for the unconverted for which we remember her.

A precious saint of God

In 1782 — when Selina's influence had reached new heights
with the opening of Spa Fields Chapel, a one-time pleasure
dome that could accommodate more than 3000 worshippers
— circumstances arose which forced her to separate from the
Church of England. After this her chapels became collectively
known as 'the Countess of Huntingdon's Connexion'. By 1789
they numbered a hundred and sixteen.

With a life spanning the greater part of the eighteenth
century, the Countess of Huntingdon had influenced virtually
all the well-known men of the revival — George Whitefield,
the Wesley brothers, Philip Doddridge, William Grimshaw,
William Romaine, John Fletcher, Henry Venn, Howell Harris,
Daniel Rowland, William Williams and many others. And
many of these men left eloquent testimony to her worth. 'The
strength of her soul is amazing', said Philip Doddridge. 'In Lady
Huntingdon I see a star of the first magnitude in the firmament
of the church', wrote Henry Venn. 'She is the most precious saint
of God I know', echoed Augustus Toplady. These men were
not mere sycophants — their comments came from a sincere
esteem as they observed the dedication of this extraordinary
woman.

My work is done

As she reached her eighties this courageous old woman could
still be found at her desk for eight hours a day, for her desire
to win the lost seemed to grow ever stronger. One who knew
her well wrote, 'Wherever a fellow creature existed, so far her
prayers extended'. With failing eyesight and spasms in her throat
that limited her to a liquid diet, the Countess toiled on. But at

almost eighty-four Selina came to the end of her pilgrimage. 'My work is done', she whispered to the doctor who attended her; 'I have nothing left to do but to go to my heavenly Father'.

On the day before she died she said repeatedly, 'I shall go to my Father this night'. And on 19 June 1791 this world lost one of its brightest exponents of Christian compassion for the souls of the lost.

Countess of Huntingdon's Chapel
Bradford on Avon

Helmsley

8. GREATLY LOVED
RICHARD CONYERS

Have you ever spent a sunny summer afternoon wandering around the picturesque market town of Helmsley in North Yorkshire? If so, you may have enjoyed sipping tea in one of the many cafés, browsing through second-hand bookshops or even savouring the exotic local ice-creams. But it would certainly add significance to any future visit to know something of the grace of God to Helmsley in the past.

Stranger to forgiveness

Dr Richard Conyers began his ministry in Helmsley parish church in 1758 — at the same time that Whitefield and the Wesley brothers were travelling the country on horseback, and William Grimshaw was preaching in Haworth and itinerating throughout Yorkshire and beyond. But when Conyers first started to preach he was himself a stranger to the grace and forgiveness of God. Unlike many of the clergy of the time, however, he was zealous and conscientious, conducting his ministry with diligence and seriousness. He did all in his power to raise standards in his parish, visiting his people and speaking privately to individuals. He even established a 'concert of prayer' for his young men, stipulating that as the clock struck a certain hour, each should find some private place and there pray, joining in spirit with the other young men of the parish.

Respected and regarded as eminently holy, Dr Conyers nevertheless grew uneasy when he read in the Scriptures, 'Woe unto you when all men speak well of you'. Certainly, he thought, these words must include him in their condemnation, for everyone held him to be a saint. But how to silence the voice of conscience, Richard Conyers did not know. Perhaps he should redouble his search for holiness. So he fasted more frequently, making solemn covenants to live unreservedly for God and sometimes signing these resolutions with his own blood.

Unsearchable riches

Nothing availed to bring Conyers relief of conscience. One day as he was reading the Scriptures in a public service of worship, he was arrested by some words in Ephesians 3 where the apostle Paul speaks of 'the unsearchable riches of Christ'. This was an entirely new concept to the troubled vicar. 'The unsearchable riches of Christ', he mused. 'I never found, I never knew, there were unsearchable riches in him'. Clearly there were depths in the Christian gospel which he had not yet plumbed. Then another thought began to distress him. If this were true, then not only was he himself in spiritual ignorance, but he had also led his people astray.

His distress heightened but still Conyers could find no answers to his fears and uncertainties. At last on Christmas Day 1758, the vicar's anxious quest ended as God dispelled the mists of his ignorance and poured the light of his truth into his soul. While he was walking slowly up to his room, two passages of Scripture flashed into his mind. One was Hebrews 9:22 — 'Without the shedding of blood there is no remission' — and the other was 1 John 1:7 — 'The blood of Jesus Christ his Son cleanses us from all sin'.

Relief and joy flooded over him, and he describes the effect: 'I went upstairs and down again, backwards and forwards in my room, clapping my hands for joy, and crying out, "I have found him — I have found him — I have found him whom my soul loveth!", and for a little time, as the Apostle said, whether in the body or out of it I could hardly tell'.

Work of grace

Helmsley Castle

Such is the account of the conversion of Richard Conyers. Speedily he invited his friends to his house to tell them of God's dealings with him. Word quickly spread of the strange things the new vicar was now saying, and the next Sunday a numerous congregation gathered to hear him. He frankly acknowledged to his astonished people that he had himself been in spiritual darkness until that very week and had misguided them in his preaching. Now he urged upon his congregation the same salvation that had brought him such assurance and peace. So began a remarkable work of grace in Helmsley as large numbers of the people were converted.

Richard Conyers soon discovered that now all did not 'speak well of him'. Anger and jealousy flared up amongst the other clergy against the earnest vicar of Helmsley, and they plotted how they might silence him. At last the Archbishop of York, hearing the many complaints, asked to hear Conyers preach. 'If he dares to preach his Methodism in the presence of his Grace', thought his antagonists, 'his gown will soon be stripped over his ears'. After his sermon the archbishop, clearly highly displeased, snapped, 'Well, Conyers, you have given us a fine sermon!' 'I am glad that I have your Grace's approbation', replied Conyers. 'Approbation! Approbation!' snorted the archbishop. 'If you go on preaching such stuff you will drive all your parish mad'.

Greatly loved

But Conyers was not intimidated, nor did the archbishop defrock him as the other clergy had hoped. Instead he continued preaching with marked success, seeing an increasing number of conversions. Whenever Whitefield or other preachers of the eighteenth-century revival were in the area, he would gladly welcome them to his pulpit, though he himself could rarely be coaxed to itinerate beyond parish bounds. So greatly was he loved by his people that when he accepted a call to Deptford in 1767 the whole town appeared to be in mourning. Many declared that they would lie across the road to prevent his carriage from leaving. In the event, Conyers had to slip away in the middle of the night to avoid the anguish of parting.

The quality of Richard Conyers' warm spiritual ministry can best be illustrated by the words of a prayer found in one of his letters to the Countess of Huntingdon: 'O thou adorable Lord Jesus, what should we talk of, or think of, or write of, or glory in but thy blessed self, who art altogether lovely! ... If we are so happy in his love when we cannot see him, Oh! what will we be when we are made like him and shall see him as he is?'

9. Devoted to Christ
Thomas Kelly

Very few Christians can trace their spiritual awakening to the reading of a Hebrew concordance of the Old Testament! But that is exactly what happened to Thomas Kelly as a twenty-two-year-old Irish law student. When he first came across the concordance (recently revised by William Romaine from an earlier edition) he was fascinated. More importantly, it led the student to seek out avidly anything he could find written by Romaine — a spiritual giant whose evangelical ministry at St Ann's in Blackfriars had been transforming London society for twenty-five years.

Thomas Kelly, only son of an Irish judge, was born in 1769 in a village not far from Athy, south-west of Dublin. Like his father, Thomas planned a career in law and had graduated with honours from Trinity College, Dublin. Pursuing legal studies at the Temple Bar in London, he came across this dry-looking Hebrew concordance — not realising that it would change his life. Before long, Romaine's writings had so influenced the young Irishman that he began to seek the Saviour to whom those writings so clearly pointed.

Path to forgiveness

Brought up in the Irish Episcopal Church, Thomas Kelly had little understanding of the gospel and struggled to please God by his upright life. But the more he tried, the greater grew his sense of failure. Long hours were spent in fasting, prayers and acts of self-denial in an attempt to gain salvation. Only when all hope of obtaining peace with God by his own merits had been stripped from him, did Thomas Kelly discover that the path to forgiveness and acceptance lay in the merits and death of Jesus Christ alone. Little wonder he could later write:

The cross! It takes our guilt away;
it holds the fainting spirit up;
it cheers with hope the gloomy day
and sweetens every bitter cup.

With new joys and aspirations burning in his heart, Kelly turned away from a career in law and began to contemplate ordination to the ministry of the Irish Episcopal Church.

But the twenty-three-year-old had a shock awaiting him when he returned home. The truths that had revolutionised his life were strenuously rejected by Kelly's own family. They could entertain no concept of forgiveness of sins apart from good works that would earn God's favour. To grieve and offend those he loved was a hard trial for the young Christian to bear. A sensitive man, Thomas Kelly declared that a martyr's death at the stake seemed a preferable option — but he did not flinch from the cost. Wherever he had opportunities, he could be found preaching the liberating truth that the sinner must be justified by faith alone in the atoning work of Christ. The cross of Christ, as Kelly had now discovered in his own experience and would later write, 'makes the coward spirit brave and nerves the feeble arm for fight'.

Rowland Hill

Not long afterwards, in 1793, Rowland Hill of Surrey Chapel, London — a battle-hardened warrior of Jesus Christ — arrived in Dublin to join Kelly in the fight. Together the two men preached at gatherings across Dublin and the people flocked to hear. But such preaching soon stirred the wrath of Archbishop Fowler of Dublin. Summoning Kelly before him, he rebuked him roundly for spreading such teachings. He issued a decree closing every Dublin pulpit to the earnest preacher. Barred from the pulpits of the Established Church, and like John Wesley, George Whitefield and others before him, Kelly began to preach wherever he could get a hearing. Before long he took the radical step of joining the ranks of the despised Dissenters.

Coming from a wealthy family (and later marrying into an equally wealthy family) Thomas Kelly consecrated all his means to the service of Christ. Before long he embarked on a chapel-building programme, erecting a number of meeting places in the villages around Dublin where people could worship Christ without state interference.

Hymns

Erudite in many fields, including oriental languages (a fact that explains his interest in a Hebrew concordance) Kelly was an earnest and lively preacher and an able Bible student. The chapels he built provided a natural outlet for his ministry, and many in that spiritually dark area had cause to thank God for his life. But today, more than 150 years after Kelly's death in 1855, the most enduring elements of his service to Christ are the hymns he wrote. A heart filled with joy will sing — and what greater reason to sing than to know one's sins are forgiven? Like Charles Wesley in England and William Williams in Wales, Kelly provided Irish Christians (and the English-speaking church) with songs to express their worship and spiritual desires.

A talented musician, with an ear for cadence and rhythm,

Thomas Kelly composed no less than 753 hymns over a period of 53 years. *Hymns on various passages of Scripture* (1804) was the first book to contain his work alone. It included 96 hymns. The last edition of that same collection, published 49 years later in 1853, incorporated all 753 that he had written.

Corporate worship

Kelly's hymns differ markedly from those of Wesley, Williams and other writers of the eighteenth-century Evangelical Revival. His chief desire seems to have been to provide hymns for the corporate worship of God's people. Although the work of Christ in his death, resurrection and triumphant ascension still lie at the heart of Kelly's compositions, the intense personal and experimental note found throughout Wesley's hymns is absent. Wesley's question, 'Died he for me, who caused his pain; for me, who him to death pursued?' would have found no place in Kelly's writings.

His lines are more objective, less experimental and less personal. This is undoubtedly a loss. Rarely does he use pronouns other than plurals such as 'we', 'us' and 'ours'. Kelly is more anxious to turn the worshipper away from himself to the glories of Christ and the progress of his kingdom. Lines like these are typical of his writing:

> *In thy name, O Lord, assembling,*
> *we thy people now draw near;*
> *teach us to rejoice with trembling;*
> *speak, and let thy servants hear;*
> *hear with meekness,*
> *hear thy word with godly fear.*

Note of triumph

John Julian's masterly work *The dictionary of hymnology*, which was first published in 1892, still stands as the final authority on any hymn written prior to his own time. He holds Thomas Kelly's work in great esteem, regarding his hymns as among the first in the English language. One that receives top accolades from Julian has these triumphant words:

The head that once was crowned with thorns
is crowned with glory now;
a royal diadem adorns
the mighty Victor's brow.

This note of triumph, aided by the bright fast-moving metres he often chose, characterises much of Kelly's work. One metre he employs to good effect is 87.87.47. William Williams had used it in 'Guide me, O thou great Jehovah', but it was Thomas Kelly who popularised it in numerous compositions:

Glory, glory everlasting
be to him who bore the cross!
who redeemed our souls, by tasting

death, the death deserved by us:
spread his glory,
who redeemed his people thus.

Exuberance and generosity

There is a robust exuberance about Kelly's work, achieved in part by the close-knit rhyming schemes he employs. His popular ascension hymn 'Look, ye saints, the sight is glorious' is a good example:

Hark, those bursts of acclamation!
Hark those loud triumphant chords!
Jesus takes the highest station:
O what joy the sight affords!
Crown him! Crown him!
King of kings and Lord of lords!

Kelly's devotion to Christ found practical expression too. During the appalling sufferings of the Irish potato famine in the mid 1840s, his generosity to the poor became a by-word. He went from home to home, saving many destitute families from disaster and death, his heart moved with pity for suffering Christians:

Poor and afflicted, yet they sing,
for Jesus is their glorious King;
through sufferings perfect now he reigns,
and shares in all their griefs and pains.

Humility

Thomas Kelly's life was marked by earnest prayerfulness, and one who knew him well said, 'Of all the humble men, he seemed to be among the most humble'. For sixty-three years this well-loved poet preached faithfully. As his life drew to a close he could declare that the truths that sustained him at the first were those on which he rested throughout his life — and they upheld him still.

Although unafraid of death, he did fear dying — lest he should dishonour his Lord in that last severe trial. But God sustained him wonderfully at the end. When someone quoted, 'The Lord is my shepherd', the dying poet interrupted saying, 'The Lord is my everything'. 'Not my will but thine be done', murmured the eighty-six-year-old Kelly just before he died.

We owe a debt of gratitude to the Irish hymn-writer for giving us some of the finest hymns in our language — hymns that have outlasted extensive changes in English usage and remain popular today.

10. No longer a slave
Amanda Smith

It was one-o'clock in the morning. A solitary figure remained still toiling in the darkened cotton fields, patiently harvesting the crop. Sam was a slave, but a slave with a difference. His master, a kindly man, had offered him the opportunity to buy his freedom. So now, by working far beyond his stated hours of service, Sam was gradually saving up the pittance he earned until he reached his own purchase price. But Sam had a further objective in view. After he had bought his own freedom he intended to buy the freedom of his wife, Mary, who worked on a neighbouring farm, and also that of his five young children.

The American Civil War would eventually lead to the legal abolition of slavery in 1865. But these were the years prior to that war, and Blacks were still despised and sometimes treated with less respect than the farm livestock. It was also a period of widespread spiritual awakening in many parts of America. Vast and noisy camp meetings were popular and on these occasions a genuine work of God could well take place, though there were also frequent scenes of spurious and emotional phenomena.

Profoundly affected

But one day an event occurred which would change the lives of Sam, Mary and their family. The only daughter of the farmer for whom Mary worked (a girl named Celie) together with a group of other young people, decided to attend a Methodist camp meeting. The young people went out of curiosity rather than concern, but the unexpected happened. Profoundly affected by the preaching, Celie was converted — a shock to her elite slave-owning family of Long Green in Madison. But shortly afterwards Celie fell ill with typhoid fever, a potential killer, and no medical skill seemed able to arrest the course of her illness. Mary, whose particular task was to care for Celie, watched over her ceaselessly, but soon it became clear that the girl had not long to live.

'I have just one request to make', said Celie to her distressed mother not long before the end. 'Anything, my dear', replied the distracted woman. 'I want you to promise me to set Mary and the children free', Celie begged. Unable to deny such a request in those painful circumstances, Celie's mother consented.

'Sing to me, Mary', the dying girl commanded the slave. In lilting tones Mary, whose own faith was simple but real, sang of the joys of the redeemed children of God in a land where slave and free alike praise the Lamb of God.

After Celie's death, her mother honoured her pledge and Mary and her children were all set free. Free they might be, but Sam and Mary quickly discovered when they moved to Pennsylvania that their privileges were few. As a god-fearing family they would pray constantly that they might find enough work to enable them to provide for the children. Black children had scant educational opportunities in those days and the eldest in the family whose name was Amanda received little more than three months schooling. An intelligent child, she was therefore largely self-taught.

At thirteen the girl was judged old enough to leave home and become a domestic servant to aid the family finances, and by seventeen she was married. Although her husband could talk freely on religious matters, Christ was not his master — in fact he was a slave to drink and Amanda's lot became an unenviable one. Disillusioned and distressed, she tried to bottle up her inner miseries. Although she came from a home where intense and warm-hearted Christian truths were regularly pressed upon her, Amanda had no personal experience of those truths. Now she did her best to hide her spiritual anxieties.

You must pray

When the girl was eighteen, however, a serious illness

threatened to spell the end of her brief life. There seemed only one answer. She must go home in order to be cared for by her own mother. But above all, Sam and Mary were anxious about the sick girl's spiritual condition. 'Amanda, my child', begged her father, 'you must pray'.

But Amanda was too ill to pray or even care. She only wanted to be left alone to die. Falling into a troubled and delirious sleep, the young woman had a strange dream. She dreamt she saw an angel standing at the foot of her bed with outspread wings. Three times the angel spoke, and each time the words were the same: 'Go back! Go back! Go back!' Perhaps God has some purpose for her life after all, thought Amanda when she woke. Slowly, very slowly, she began to recover.

When she was well enough Amanda returned to her husband, but so close a brush with death had brought a new seriousness into her life. Still self-willed and proud, however, she laid down conditions under which she would accept God's mercy. Yet in spite of this she became increasingly aware of her sin, and always Satan whispered, 'God will never hear your prayers. You're such a sinner'. 'True', thought Amanda. 'But if only I knew of someone who had obeyed God perfectly and had never sinned.

Then he could pray for me, and God would hear him'. Although there is One who 'makes intercession for transgressors', in her ignorance and the blindness of unbelief, Amanda began to address inanimate objects — the sun, the moon, the stars, the trees. 'Sun', she would say, 'you have never sinned like me. You have always obeyed God and kept your place in the heavens. Tell Jesus I am a poor sinner'.

Inner battle

But the sun did not pray for her. At last Amanda became desperate. She must receive an answer from God or die. By now she was nineteen and working as a housemaid in a Columbia home. So, after fulfilling all her duties one afternoon, Amanda went downstairs to the cellar. Here she determined she would stay until God heard her cry. Otherwise the family would have to come down and discover her dead body. At last she realised that her only hope lay in finding the grace of God through Christ for herself.

'Oh Lord', she cried out in desperation as she knelt in lonely vigil; 'I have come down here to die. I must either have salvation or death this afternoon. Oh! if you will only convert my soul and make me to know it'. How long the inner battle raged she could not tell. Amanda had no more words left with which to plead her case. She just looked up and waited. Then at last she prayed, 'If you will help me, I will believe you'. This was the prayer of faith — a prayer that brings joy in heaven.

Amanda sprang to her feet — she felt a new woman. She looked at her hands. Yes, they were still black hands, but they seemed quite new. She felt new all over; a new creation in Christ. She ran up the cellar stairs to the kitchen to view herself in a mirror to see if the glory in her soul had altered her face.

Alone

In vain Satan tried to sow his seeds of doubt in Amanda's mind during the days that followed. 'Though I have passed through many sorrows, many trials, never have I had a question in regard to my conversion', she afterwards declared. And many trials there were. The death of her infant son occurred soon after that lonely spiritual conflict in the cellar. Then came the death of her husband who had all but forsaken Amanda in any case. He had enlisted with the Confederate army when the Civil War broke out. All alone except for a young daughter called Mazie, Amanda urgently needed more work and soon drifted back to Philadelphia in search of better employment. Here she met a minister of religion, James Smith, a man of high religious pretensions. 'The Rev. and Mrs James Smith', she thought to herself. That sounds grand. And before long Amanda embarked on a second marriage, but one that proved as disastrous as the first, for James was a hypocrite.

Ill-treated and neglected, Amanda's faith wavered as trials, sorrows and poverty seemed to dog her path. The death of a five-month old baby, followed shortly afterwards by that of James himself, left her weak and ill. But God had purposes for Amanda's life and his care was over her. Gradually she regained physical and spiritual strength.

Triumphant testimony

With none of her own left apart from Mazie, now a teenager, Amanda felt God's call to a life of active Christian service. First came tract distribution, then there followed requests to sing at the crowded camp meetings, and finally opportunities to address groups of those who had gathered there.

This in turn led to yet wider travels as she received pressing invitations to tell of God's dealings with her soul. By the mid 1870s Amanda could be found far from her home: Africa, India and even England. Many who heard her triumphant testimony of God's dealings with a poor girl, born into slavery, glorified God for the life of one freed from bondage to labour for a Master whose service is perfect liberty.

11. SERVING TIRELESSLY
FRED MITCHELL

A young prisoner was hustled through the massive entrance gates of Wormwood Scrubbs and quickly pushed into a cell. The heavy door slammed behind him and Fred Mitchell was left alone. What had the open-faced boy from Yorkshire done to deserve such a punishment? It was 1915 and the First World War was not going well for England. At the Battle of Ypres that August thousands of men had died from the fearsome effects of chlorine gas, used against them for the first time.

Fred Mitchell, an earnest Christian youth, was a Conscientious Objector. Although he had joined a non-combatant corps, he soon felt that to be loading up guns in readiness for others to fire was little different from firing them himself. He could not go on. And one day he disobeyed orders, and refused any further compliance. Court-martialled, he was sentenced to spend the rest of the war in prison. Although with maturing years he would change his view on armed combat, Fred early learnt the cost of remaining true to his principles.

Are you saved?

Jackson Bridge where Fred was born in 1897 is a small village south of Huddersfield. From a Methodist family, Fred was a cocksure but intelligent lad, and at thirteen won a scholarship to a well-reputed local grammar school. But although he attended church services regularly and sang in the choir, Fred and his close friend Walter were astonished when a local mill worker thrust a tract into their hands with the searching question, 'Are you saved?' Of course they were saved, Fred assured Walter. But Walter was troubled. Day after day the two sixteen-year-olds would meet on the station as they travelled to work in Huddersfield, where Fred was now training as a pharmacist. Each time Walter would ask, 'Are you really sure we are saved?' Gradually Fred was not so sure. So they decided to visit the mill worker one night to find out how to be certain that they were saved.

With all the skill of a true soul winner, the mill worker took the boys from scripture to scripture until they were convinced of their desperate state as sinners. Only when they were deeply concerned did he point them to the Saviour, forsaken by God on the cross for their sins. As Fred was later to write, 'It was as if a blind had been drawn up in my soul. The light streamed in. I was saved and knew it. Hallelujah!' The same was true for Walter, as both stood at the dawn of a lifetime's service for Jesus Christ. At every opportunity the boys would distribute tracts near their homes, speaking to any who might listen.

The call of China

But now in the isolation of a Wormwood Scrubbs prison cell, Fred had a unique chance to study his Bible. Like John Bunyan, he learnt more of his God during those prison days than ever before. After a year he was transferred to a work centre in Wakefield where he was given his liberty, but required to perform many uncongenial tasks throughout the war. During this time Fred Mitchell came across a book that 'stirred my youthful soul to the depths' and would profoundly affect the course of his life — *A thousand miles of miracle in China* by A. E. Glover. The book tells of the sufferings of Christian missionaries through the fearsome days of the Boxer riots in 1900. Hunted mercilessly like wild animals, they were tortured and killed. A new ambition grew in Fred's heart — he would go to China to help fill the depleted ranks of those brave missionaries.

But a new trouble hit the family in 1918. Fred's father was struck down in the devastating flu epidemic that killed more people than the World War itself. This made Fred responsible for his widowed mother, and the prospect of going to China faded, although the hope did not. Now a qualified pharmacist, Fred was chosen from among fifty applicants to manage a chemist shop in Bradford. And here the twenty-two-year- old would remain for the next fourteen years. Upright and efficient, he conducted his business affairs with competence. But his heart was faraway in China — a land he now feared he might never see. 'When I am dead,' he once said, 'you will find China written on my heart'. His marriage in 1922 to Nellie Hey, an earnest Christian girl, added further problems, for at that time Nellie could hardly bear to contemplate life in China.

Regular preaching

Although Fred Mitchell might not be able to go, he could still serve the country of his desires. During the following years he established prayer meetings in Bradford and in many surrounding areas to support the labours of missionaries in China. Nor was he a mere dreamer of idle dreams. What about the needs of Bradford itself? With the help of the pastor of the Sunbridge Road Mission, which Fred Mitchell was soon to join, he threw all his efforts into evangelisation among the needy of the city. Before long he also started annual meetings after the model of the Keswick Convention to encourage local Christians.

Fred was not just an activist — he backed up all his undertakings with an ever-growing communion with his Lord as he constantly endeavoured to become more godly. A great reader, the young chemist immersed himself not only in such classics as The Life of Hudson Taylor (by Dr and Mrs Howard Taylor) but in a wide range of Christian literature. A volume of The Letters of Samuel Rutherford was among his favourites.[1]

In 1932 Fred, who now had three children to support, took the bold step of purchasing his own chemist shop. Gloomy friends predicted that he would fail, for Bradford had numerous chemist shops already. But with diligence and standards of excellence, Fred Mitchell — Chemist became the leading pharmacist in Bradford. And Fred dispensed more than medicines, for many came through his doors with pressing spiritual or social needs, and the busy chemist had time for all.

In addition Fred maintained a regular preaching schedule; he kept in constant touch with the China Inland Mission headquarters in London, becoming a member of the London

Council of the mission. Nor did he neglect his growing family. But one day early in 1942 a letter with a London postmark arrived on the Mitchells' doormat — one that would change Fred's life. It was an invitation to succeed as the new Home Director of the CIM — a staggering proposition.

Fulfilment

Fred hesitated long. How could he fulfil such a responsibility? He had not even been to China. At last it was Nellie who became convinced that this was God's will — even though it meant uprooting her family. With humble dependence on his God, the stocky Yorkshire businessman set about his new responsibilities at Newington Green in north London. Accustomed to consulting no one in his business decisions, he made a number of initial mistakes, but gradually learnt to work in co-operation with others.

Then came the fulfilment of his heart's desire — a visit to China in 1947. So long had he 'lived' there in imagination that the sights appeared familiar — although riding on horseback through rushing rivers and along precipitous mountain ledges was almost more than the staid Yorkshireman could handle. But establishing warm friendships with many missionaries brought untold joy to Fred.

No sooner was he back before a further responsibility devolved on this unpretentious man — an invitation to become Chairman of the Keswick Convention. The support and friendship of Dr Lloyd-Jones was a great encouragement at this demanding time. Though coming from a different theological perspective, Lloyd-Jones recognised in Mitchell a kindred spirit. They shared a love of books and were one in spiritual desires and endeavour. Gradually 'the Doctor' was drawn into the work of the Mission, and his advice was invaluable. For these were traumatic days

as the Communist take-over of China in 1949 brought about a
watershed in the Mission's life.

Mitchell was at the helm as that sad withdrawal of all
personnel took place in 1951 — and he was among those who
oversaw the placement of missionaries in the new fields of
South East Asia to which the Mission now turned. 'Have faith
in God' was the text carved in stone above the entrance to the
Mission headquarters. How often must Fred Mitchell have
glanced up at it when a blackbird built its nest over the word
'faith' in May 1951.

Climbing on track

Less than two years later in April 1953 the fifty-five year-old
Home Director paid a visit to Malaysia to see how the work was
developing. A strange desire to urge his hearers to persevere to
the end seemed to characterise Fred's ministry. Twice he preached
on 'I have fought a good fight, I have finished my course ...'
With the hectic schedule of meetings and consultations at last
complete, Fred prepared to fly home from Singapore. His flight
was booked on the Comet — the first ever commercial jet aircraft,
built by de Havilland Aircraft and in service just one year. It could
carry only 37 passengers but flew at the then phenomenal speed
of 475 mph. Landing in Bangkok, Fred disembarked for a few
moments and spoke to waiting missionaries, 'We have pledged
ourselves to go forward ... we must expect severe testing'.

A pilot with a flying record of a million miles was in the
cockpit, and as the powerful aircraft roared out of Calcutta, he
sent a reassuring message, 'Climbing on track ...'. Then nothing.
All contact was lost. The next day the astonishing news flashed
around the world that the much-vaunted Comet had been found
smashed to pieces, lying in a paddy field twenty-two miles from

Calcutta. There were no survivors. Stunned, Christians worldwide could scarcely take in the news. Some months later two
other Comets crashed, and it was eventually found that a design
fault had led to fatigue cracking in the pressurised cabin.

But Dr Lloyd-Jones spoke straight to the heart of the grieving
Mission and its friends at a memorial service on 26 May 1953.
'There are no accidents in the case of God's children ... God
cannot make mistakes. Why? Because he is the Lord — his ways
are always perfect'.

Footnote

[1] I once possessed Fred Mitchell's own copy of this book, and
his careful underlining shows the depth of his appreciation.